T0114874

WALKING WITH GOD AND MY DOG

A Spiritual Journey

HEATHER BENNETT

WESTBOW
PRESS®
A DIVISION OF THOMAS NELSON
& ZONDERVAN

WestBow Press books may be ordered through booksellers or by contacting:

WestBow Press
A Division of Thomas Nelson & Zondervan
1663 Liberty Drive
Bloomington, IN 47403
www.westbowpress.com
844-714-3454

ISBN: 978-1-6642-1956-4 (sc)
ISBN: 978-1-6642-1957-1 (e)

Library of Congress Control Number: 2021900871

Print information available on the last page.

WestBow Press rev. date: 02/11/2021

"We have never reaped such a harvest from seed as much as from that which fell from our hearts while tears fell from our eyes." - Charles Spurgeon

DEDICATION

To the love of my life, Malcolm, who gave me two beautiful children and four grandchildren, and who is "still the one". Thanks be to God for showing us how to walk through this life with Him at the helm.

CONTENTS

Why Me, God?

In 2002, I began writing in my spiritual journal about walking with God and my dog, Monty. I started recording all the ways God had spoken to me with visions and whisperings during those walks in the woods, which were followed by my praises and prayers. Then God impressed on my heart that I should share them, to bring hope and encouragement to others.

You might ask, why so long? There were the usual excuses and delays. Write a book? Me? Are you crazy, God? No one will want to read a book about my experiences! But God said (I say that phrase frequently in this book), "This isn't about you, Heather."

Have you ever tried to say no to God? Jonah did and look where he ended up (in the belly of a whale). Over the years I have received gentle nudging and further visions to record as my faith has grown. God kept asking me, "Are you ready now?" And I kept saying, "I can't do this". Disappointing and disobeying God makes my heart break, so I put my head down (in prayer) and my pen to paper, and sought God's help. He kept reminding me that I was not alone and that this was His story. "His loving-kindness is from everlasting to everlasting" (Psalm 103:17 NIV).

In the fall of 2011, I had to put down my faithful companion, Monty, due to cancer of the mouth. It was on Black Friday and it truly was a dark, sad day. My husband and I buried him in the woods, where I had walked with him; it was his favorite place. Monty was a beautiful, smart, faithful, and loving Sheltie. He had been a gift to my young daughters and me during a marital separation and impending divorce. My husband chose this breed because he knew that I had always wanted one. He brought the girls with him to pick it out, and Monty was the first puppy to come over to them and lick their faces all over. He was so full of unconditional love, which was exactly what we all needed at the time.

One of my favorite scriptures is Psalm 116:6 (NASB) which says, "…I was brought low, and He saved me." This was from 1982 - my first year as a newlywed. My husband and I became born again and were baptized together. We attended a local church and began our family life there. The church began to have problems, and we drifted away without finding a new church or staying and trying to improve things. This was a big mistake. It was a result of our immaturity in life and as new Christ followers. We walked back into the world for solace and answers.

Over a five-year period we fought, made up, and tried secular counseling. I was the first to stray from our marriage, looking for happiness. Happiness did not come, and we ended up in a stinky ash pile instead of in the marriage God had designed for us. We both thought divorce was the only relief for ourselves and our daughters, who had unfortunately been exposed to our fights and our misery.

This is when I came back to God. I returned to my Christian faith in a passionate way, and found that He was waiting for me with open arms. I truly identify with the woman caught in adultery and Jesus saving her from being stoned by telling those men, "Let any one of you who is without sin, be the first to throw a stone at her"(John 8:7 NIV). Oh, how I could wash His feet with my tears and dry them with my hair like she did. Jesus explains this beautifully in Luke 7:47 (NIV), which says, "Therefore, I tell you, her many sins have been forgiven-as her great love has shown. But whoever has been forgiven little loves little." At a point when I felt that Jesus was all that I had, I realized that He was all that I needed. Jesus became my counselor, my friend, and even a replacement for my husband.

During this time, I found a new church, which became a home and a place to grow and serve God. Serving God is the best way to take your focus off your own problems and receive peace and comfort. I wore a path to the altar, praying for my girls and our future. My girls were sixteen and thirteen by that time, and I hoped I was not too late to help them find the importance of God in their lives.

My husband had moved out and had begun a new life with someone he believed was his soulmate. As painful as this was (she was nearly twenty years my junior), I was relieved in some respects. I had been unable to make him happy in our almost twenty years of marriage, and I was tired of trying. I won't say that this was easy. When you join your life in marriage with someone and become one, dissolving it feels like half your heart is ripped out of your chest. Many times, I hugged the Word of God to my heart (literally and figuratively) for comfort.

This all came to a head in August of that year and my birthday was in September. That is when we got Monty. I accepted the gift reluctantly from my husband but he insisted that it was a gift from my girls to me. I also hoped Monty would bring them some comfort during our divorce. Little did I know how much he would mean to me. Monty, known for his affectionate and loyal ways, became my constant walking companion. Whether in my neighborhood or in the woods where we spent most of our time, he was always by my side. He never needed a leash because he never strayed far from me. People I came across were amazed at how good he was and what a mama's boy he was. Whether I was at home reading my Bible or in the woods crying and praying, he was always there. And so was God.

My heart was broken and God filled it with His love and purpose. Monty's unconditional love and faithfulness was in step with my Lord and savior, Jesus Christ. I hope this comparison and the title of my book does not offend whoever may read it. God and dog just made so much sense to me. When I thought about God, the creator of the world including man's best friend, I decided to continue with the title. I believe God smiles at the whimsical title, and I know He gave me the idea. So while this book is a collection of experiences that I had with God and my dog in the woods, it is mostly the story of God's hand in the healing of my marriage and family. My God is an awesome God, and I want to give Him all the honor, glory, praise and thanks for this miracle.

2

Pine Needles

One of the first times I felt God's presence I was walking through a pine grove. It was one of my daily walks with Monty. The sun was warm and causing the air to fill with a soothing aroma from the fallen pine needles. It reminded me of happier days with my husband when we were young and in love. It made me suddenly feel very sad, lonely, and ugly, thinking about my bleak future as a divorcee.

Then suddenly, in my heart, or soul, or mind, or all three, I heard, "You are beautiful to me.

I am here." A feeling of love and overwhelming acceptance surrounded me. What peace, hope, and joy! God thought I was beautiful, and He was not going to forsake me ever! His love is unconditional and I don't need a leash for Him either. The great "I Am" would be there for me. This has been true to this day!

During our separation I couldn't eat much. The food seemed to stick in my craw. Because of my weight loss, my primary care doctor wanted to put me on antidepressants. We discussed giving up coffee for my stomach issues and giving up alcohol because of its depressive effects. She agreed to allow this, and it worked.

Occasionally I took antacids, but mostly I gorged on the Word of God. I read it, researched it, spoke it out loud, and even wrote every Psalm in a notebook. I slept with my Bible hugged close to my heart and used scriptures that I had memorized to battle the attacks I sometimes had in the night when I would awaken in fear.

During this time I listened to only Christian music. I went up to the altar at church so many times that I think I wore a path in the carpet. Once, I even went to a healing priest and asked for prayer for my husband and the priest said, "Love him." I ended up on the floor (slain in the spirit). I prayed, and I groaned when I couldn't pray. Often I called a sister in Christ when I felt really weak. I continued in Christian counseling and attended church regularly, absorbing good teaching. I sought other Christian books, as God led me, that addressed the changes I needed to make in myself. These included studies on seeking my significance in God, seeking joy in all circumstances, forgiveness, and battling the evil one.

Church attendance was crucial and I want to

thank my wonderful Pastor and the whole body of Christ for enveloping me at this time. There were opportunities to serve that took me out of my own problems. The church had a building project and I found healing in mudding dry wall. I joined a group that visited nursing homes with music and encouragement. Serving others is a great way to take the focus off yourself.

My daughters were dragged along with me, as I hoped to change the direction of their futures. I began praying for them, including their future vocations and husbands. God has answered these prayers with wonderful sons-in-laws and daughters happy with what they have chosen to do in life.

I continued walking every day with God and my dog Monty. I walked in faith not by sight. My prayer became that I would be a pleasing aroma to Him in whatever He had planned for me. Like those pine needles are a pleasing aroma to me, my life can be a pleasing aroma to God. This idea of being a pleasing aroma to God came to me again on a motorcycle trip years later. During a morning church service at a motorcycle rally in Pennsylvania, the Pastor asked us to share something that God had shared with us recently. I spoke about smelling the aroma of Timothy grass being harvested on my ride to the rally, and how it made me smile and thank God. That smell is heavenly to me, and I was reminded that my life and my actions can be an aroma to God. I asked myself if I wanted my aroma to be a stench or something pleasing. Bad attitudes and evil motives are a stink to God. A pure heart and clean hands are not.

The gentlemanly Holy Spirit of God can be grieved and turn away from us when we sin. I determined at that time that I never wanted to be without my friend and counselor, the Holy Spirit. When I felt myself going down the wrong path I became jealous of my relationship with Him, and did not like the feeling of His lost presence. I did not want Him to turn from an unpleasing aroma, as we humans do. I wanted to put a smile on His face, as He often does for me. My prayer for this book, is that it will be a pleasing aroma to Him and a comfort or help to someone out there that may read it.

3

Wild Flowers

One day while walking with a heavy heart on a dreary spring morning, I was particularly burdened by my daughters' absent relationship with their father. Their relationship had deteriorated with the awareness of the new woman in their Dad's life. They had been resigned to our separation, and had been excited about helping him set up his new apartment. But, after finding evidence of this new person, they were angry. They refused to see him and even told him not to come to their soccer games. My husband and I both knew how exceptionally vulnerable they would be as teenagers without a good father-daughter relationship.

Being at a loss about how or what to pray, I started praying in tongues (a gift from the Holy Spirit). I know some people do not believe in this phenomenon, but it has become a regular part of my prayer life. All I want to say about this subject is don't knock it until you have tried it. You can ask for this gift, as I did. I do not do it in front of other people. It is between me and God.

Well, as I was walking, weeping, and praying in this way, a light rain began to fall. I kept walking for almost an hour when I came to a sharp turn in the trail that caused me to stop and look around. The sun suddenly broke through the clouds and was shining through the trees. In front of me was a tall, wide expanse of weeds, and among them was a small cluster of four yellow flowers. The sun illuminating those four flowers was beautiful and eerie. Then came God's presence again, impressing on me "This is your family. It represents your husband, you, and your daughters." The great I Am (that great I Am, again) was going to restore my family! The great I Am was going "...to bestow on them a crown of beauty instead of ashes..." (Isaiah 61:3 NIV).

What? Are you crazy, Lord? Monty did you hear that?

But again came the flood of peace, hope, and joy. This flooded my heart, mind, and soul. God gave me a vision that I would struggle to hold on to for months and years to come. It makes me think of Joseph in the book of Genesis, getting the vision of his father and brothers bowing down to him, which didn't happen for many years and trials to come. He mistakenly shared it with them and they made fun of him. I did not share my vision with anyone because it seemed so implausible.

I was in good company, I guess. Also from the book of Genesis, Abraham was given a promise of an heir, but waited many years for it to come to pass. He and his wife Sarah tried to help God out, tried to move things along faster, because they were tired of waiting. This is never a wise choice. God doesn't need your help but I understand the temptation. It is hard to wait.

Not long after that, my Christian counselor shared with me a vision that she received while praying before our counseling session. She saw me in the future, holding a cup which would "runneth over" with blessings, as it says in Psalm 23:5 (KJV).

As I pondered this vision or promise, I began to see God's wisdom. Though I had been relieved to let my husband go thinking maybe she could make him happy where I could not, I began to see that he was not happy and he never would be without a relationship with his girls. I also believed he would never be happy without a restored relationship with God.

My new path began, a path of becoming a "redeemer" in my marriage (a term from a sermon by Jimmy Evans), and with a new goal of *Taking Back What the Devil Stole* (the title of a book by Joyce Meyers). God had forgiven me of my adultery and struggles with pornography. Pornography is widely accepted in this culture, but I have come to believe it is a form of adultery in itself, and sometimes can lead to unfaithfulness in relationships.

So I began praying for my husband, praying for the other woman (very difficult, by the way), and praying for reconciliation, regeneration, and renewal. These are God's specialties! My husband was on his own spiritual journey, and began to realize that he still had feelings for me. He did not have a lot of hope, but he had feelings despite my hurting him. He saw a change in me and began going to the same Christian counselor as me. We went separately at first, until eventually she felt we should go together.

At this point, I want to encourage any struggling believer to seek good Christian counseling. We had tried secular counseling earlier in our marriage, but it did not help and might have even made things worse. I do not mean to disparage good secular counselors, but I prefer someone who has the Almighty God and His word in their bag of knowledge.

Back to my story. Eventually my husband's girlfriend moved out at his request, but she was reluctant to move out of his life. And he still cared for her. I did not understand or like this, but God gave me a vision in answer to that as well. (see the Old Leaves chapter) Like I said, waiting on God can be hard, but it is always worth it.

Gradually my daughters and my husband began to heal their relationships, but my daughters were thoroughly against us getting back together. My flesh was in agreement with the sentiment, but God was dealing with me as well. More walking with God and my dog needed to be done on that one!

4

Dead Log

How could this marriage be healed, you may ask? I asked myself the same question, and I couldn't see a way. Can God make a way where there appears to be no way? He did it for the Israelites escaping slavery in Egypt by parting the Red Sea so they could cross on dry ground! I will have to trust and believe in Him. In my flesh and weakling human mind I could not imagine getting beyond what we had done to each other. I asked God, "How can we get over all this rottenness?"

Monty and I have a favorite trail. He is actually now buried on that trail. Near where he is buried is a huge rock, where I always pause to pray, and often climb to the top of. I call it Praise Rock, because I stand at the top with my hands lifted high praising God for whatever comes to mind, such as: the fresh air, the beautiful sunshine, the sound of birds, my salvation, His great love for me, and His plans for me and my family. When I climb down I try not to doubt God's promises, because I have learned you cannot be double-minded with God. You cannot pray in faith, and then speak doubt.

While hiking one day not far from Praise Rock, I came upon a tree that had another dead tree crushed against it, bending it over. Succumbing to an urge, I pushed it off and it fell to the opposite side of the trail. God quickened my heart to understand that this is what would happen to the rottenness that had happened in our marriage, and the resultant baggage. "Push it away" He said, and don't dwell on it. Focus on the healthy and good part of your marriage, the good memories, and your future hope. Reach for the sunlight, and start growing again together.

I am not making light of this and saying it was an easy process. There were many tears, deep conversations, and counseling sessions, but ultimately God healed the wounds and made us healthy again. I still saw the remnants of that rotten log for years after on my walks, but now after almost 20 years it is gone. The tree that had been crushed has grown through the canopy of trees to reach the sun. My husband and I reach for the Son of God by loving each other, growing in our faith, serving in our church, and praising Him for all our blessings. We are so thankful for God giving us "beauty for ashes" in our marriage and in our relationship with our children, and for planting us in a wonderful church. We willingly share our story with others that we may remain humble, and perhaps bring hope to those struggling.

5

Old Leaves

In a previous chapter, I promised to tell you about "old leaves" which is probably my favorite vision from God. Some people might think I made this stuff up on my walks with Monty, but I am not smart enough to think of this one on my own. Hahaha!

As I mentioned in a previous chapter, the "other woman" was reluctant to move on with her life without my husband. My husband felt bad for causing her unhappiness, but I wasn't as sympathetic. God had prompted me to pray for her on a regular basis, but that was not easy. At first I could only pray for her as an enemy. Scripture says if you are kind towards your enemy and pray for him "you will heap burning coals on his head" (Proverbs 25:22 NIV). This does not sound very nice, but it was a start for me. Eventually, I could say her name and began to have compassion for her. This is probably part of God's plan. When He calls us to pray for our enemies, it softens our heart. She had obviously become entangled in our mess and had gotten injured by it. But I wanted her to go away, and I wanted her to stop caring for my husband. And I especially wanted him to stop caring for her!

Walking with Monty on a cold blustery day, I was pouring out my anguish before God. King David did this in the Psalms, which was my example. Remember, I had written the whole of Psalms in a notebook, word for word. I love how

David spews all his frustrations and fears before God, but eventually comes to his senses and remembers God's goodness and sovereignty. What is great about this example, is that God is OK with our rants and hearing about our pain. He loves us. He is a good, good father. Don't we embrace our children when they are hurting? So does our Almighty Father. His "…lovingkindness …is from everlasting to everlasting…" (Psalm 103:17 NASB).

So I was walking and crying and venting, asking questions. "How is this going to work God?" "How can I make them stop caring for one another?" My husband had reassured me numerous times that he loved me and wanted our marriage to succeed, but he still cared what happened to her. He was honest, and I give him credit for that, but it still made me physically ill to think about it. "Help me Lord, I cannot do this in my own flesh!", I prayed.

I had chosen a little used trail because of my tears and distress. I did not want to encounter any other walkers because they would think I was a crazy, distraught person. Carefully descending a steep, snowy hill as the wind whipped through the trees, I came upon an amazing sight. Most of the trees had shed their leaves by this time, but I came upon a stand of trees that still had dry leaves, clinging and fluttering madly in the wind. I thought how odd this was, and that I would have to research what kind of trees they were when I got home (beech trees by the way). They had beautiful whitish-beige leaves and were fascinating to watch, which stopped me in my tracks, and also stopped my ranting emotions.

I pondered my painful struggle and the desire I had for the feelings that they had for each other to stop. Could I do anything to make it stop, Lord? The great I Am, spoke to my heart, "Look at these leaves and trees I have created. Only new growth will push the old leaves off. Patience my daughter, just love your husband, and the new growth will push off the old." Again, I say Wow! Thank you, Lord. I can do that. I can love him. I do love him.

Needless to say, I checked those leaves over that long, cold, New England winter, my faithful dog, Monty, braving the elements with me. Despite the wind, snow, ice, and rain the leaves hung on. And then as spring came, I watched as they were finally pushed off by the new growth.

There were many other times God spoke to me and encouraged me when I would fall back into old pitfalls and bad attitudes. It is easy to fall back into a rut caused by years of dysfunction. But "the word of God is alive and active. Sharper than any two edged sword..." (Hebrews 4:12 NIV). And it is a great tool to battle our human weaknesses. It can correct, as well as encourage us, and is the reason we should be in it daily. It is our daily bread and we should go to it when we are hungry for an answer.

My beloved pastor, Phil, once preached on this topic, and I agree wholeheartedly with his message. He said when you have a problem find out what the Bible says about it. Read it out loud, and memorize a verse that speaks to your heart and encourages you.

I especially enjoy reading the Psalms out loud. King David had many problems in his life, but he was still a man after Gods own heart. Ask others to pray for and with you. Seek God in prayer, even if it's just in groans or one word prayers. Believe the best and don't speak the worst about a person or situation.

One verse that encouraged me during that time was Romans 15:13 (NASB95), "Now may the God of hope fill you with all joy and peace in believing, so that you will abound in hope by the power of the Holy Spirit." I reminded myself that there is "joy and peace in believing" whenever doubt or fear came my way. As believers in Christ, we were not given a spirit of fear. That is from the evil one. I cut down that root of fear whenever it tried to grow back, with the word of God.

Eventually it stopped trying to grow back. "Resist the devil and he will flee from you" (James 4:7 NIV). Fear is something I had to deal with my whole life. The word of God finally gave me a weapon to fight it. I would hack it down with the sword of the Spirit! This visual of the root of fear trying to re-sprout was from God as well. He showed me how to stop it from regrowing, an amazing power that He provides us with.

I recall one of the last times fear came at me in a big way. After a year of reconciliation with my husband, she had finally moved on and taken a job elsewhere. I breathed a sigh of relief, but that was a mistake. One day, he took a motorcycle ride to see her, and then he confessed it to me. I was surprised at what welled up in my spirit. I firmly told God that I was done and wanted to walk away. Hadn't I been through enough? Hadn't I believed and loved like He told me to? I said, "I cant believe anymore, Lord. I can't trust him!"

But God said, "You don't have to trust him. Trust Me!"

Bam! How can I argue with that? But, I still did argue, until the following day when a Christian friend gave me a jewelry box from a trip she had just returned from. It was a gift for watching her dog. It was inscribed with, "Love bears all things, believes all things, hopes all things, endures all things" (1Corinthians 13:7 ESV). It reminded me to get back in the battle against my fear and doubt. There have been other small skirmishes since then, but I try not to forget the spiritual weapons in my arsenal. Scripture reminds me, "…the one who is in you is greater than the one that is in the world." (1 John 4:4 NIV).

6

Beyond!

Years later, I was asked to tell my story at a woman's retreat. It was a story of God's ability to take us beyond our pasts, beyond our failures, and beyond our dreams. I want to make one thing clear, God is good but that does not mean He is like a slot machine. You cannot just send up a prayer and expect immediate results. God is about relationship and He wants to spend time with you. Getting to know Him in your wilderness experience is the best part of any suffering you are going through. I would not exchange the relationship I have with Him for anything, even if I could erase the trial my family went through.

The big temptation is to pray for our circumstances to change or for someone else to change. But God is focused on you. He may want you to change an attitude or behavior. We must praise and worship Him, in spite of our mood or circumstances. A dear sister in Christ once told me, "I love you, and I will pray for you, but it is time to turn this pity party into a praise party!" Praising God when things are difficult will lift your spirit more than you can imagine.

Romans 5:3-5 (NIV) says, "And not only this, but we also exult in our tribulations, knowing that tribulation brings about perseverance; and perseverance, proven character; and proven character, hope; and hope does not disappoint, because the love of God has been poured out within our hearts through the Holy Spirit who was given to us." There is a whole message in this verse alone. Joy in our troubles you may ask? Joyce Meyers is famous for a robot routine on stage. She stiffly marches around like a robot saying, "What about me, what about me?" She says people always ask "why" and "when" in their trials. "Why" did this happen to me? "When" will it be over? I will never forget her instruction to change it to "what" and "how". "What can I learn from this, God?" "How can I bring you glory, God?"

So, Romans says that joy in our troubles produces perseverance and patience? Well, think about children getting everything they ask for. Is that good parenting? Children that can hear "no" and "wait" do better in adulthood. The same applies in the spiritual realm. Patience produces character that other people can see. Many people, both Christian and non-Christian, thought I was crazy or foolish to believe my marriage could survive. There were times when my flesh was apt to agree, but I had that vision from God deep in my heart.

No one likes pain. Does a bush like being pruned? I love to prune, and my husband worries that sometimes I may kill what I am pruning. Being pruned by the hand of God may appear like that as well. Undergoing life's difficulties is uncomfortable, and we want it to be over. But God knows what He is doing, looking forward to the beautiful outcome, the beautiful bloom that will result in the future.

The winter after I had lost Monty, I was walking alone past his grave. I was in great despair after a conflict between my husband and youngest daughter over her wedding plans. It seemed like an impossible situation with two very powerful wills clashing, and I could do little but pray. The day matched my mood, as it was frigid, windy, and cloudy. Without Monty, I felt alone and sad as I crunched through the snow. I couldn't climb up Praise Rock because of the snow and ice, so I climbed up a ridge beyond it to seek God in comfort. As I stood there among the trees, the sun suddenly appeared and there were beautiful little birds flying all around me. They flitted from tree to tree, seemingly as excited to see the sun as I was. A smile spread across my face as I felt the presence of God and a reassurance that I was not alone. God's word "And the peace of God, which passeth all understanding" (Philippians 4:7 KJ) filled my heart and I released my worries unto Him.

In time, my husband wrote a beautiful letter of submission to his daughter, which touched her heart. The wedding was beautiful and blessed. Character produces hope, and this hope will never disappoint as God fills our hearts with love through His Holy Spirit. Remember that you are never alone!

In conclusion my friends, never stop learning from, and listening to God. Learn to feed yourself from His word. What I mean by this is don't always live like an infant having to be fed by others. And to those who are married or will be someday, don't gossip or slander your husband, for this "uncovers" him and ultimately opens your marriage up for attack. Meet with one Christian friend or counsellor for prayer and guidance. Fight your battles with prayer, and always remember that God is the third person in your marriage if you have taken your vows before Him. God loves your spouse more than you do, and He has a vision for your future. "For I know the plans that I have for you, declares the Lord, plans to prosper you and not to harm you, plans to give you hope and a future." (Jeremiah 29:11 NIV).

Amen.

PROLOGUE

"If your law had not been my delight, I would have perished in my affliction."

(Psalm 119:92 NIV).

Psalm 119 is the longest Psalm and my favorite. I love this whole Psalm, and I read it aloud whenever I feel dry in my faith, or far from God's presence. When I feel this way, it's usually of my own doing, not His, for the Holy Spirit is always present. Sometimes we turn away from Him or our sin grieves Him.

Today in November of 2019, as I completed this story, I was touched by this scripture from Corinthians 2:10-13 (NIV), "these things God has revealed to us through the Spirit. For the Spirit searches everything, even the depths of God. For who knows a person's thoughts except the spirit of that person, which is in him? So also no one comprehends the thoughts of God except the Spirit of God. Now we have received not the spirit of the world, but the Spirit who is from God, that we might understand the things freely given us by God. And we impart this in words not taught by human wisdom but taught by the Spirit, interpreting spiritual truths to those who are spiritual."

I am hoping and praying that this book was written with the help of the Holy Spirit, and speaks only God's truths. To God be the glory. There have been many other examples of visions from God in my life, but I chose the ones related to my healed family and the ones I had with Monty. Someday if prompted by the Holy Spirit, I may write again. Thank you for reading, and God bless you.

~ Heather

Printed in the United States
By Bookmasters